For the Love of God

The Sacred Heart and The Divine Mercy

Kristina Olsen, PhD, DBA, OCDS

En Route Books and Media, LLC

Saint Louis, MO

⊕*ENROUTE*
Make the time

En Route Books and Media, LLC
5705 Rhodes Avenue
St. Louis, MO 63109

Cover credit: After Adolf Hyla, Painting of the Divine Mercy, Archives of the Congregation of the Sisters of Our Lady of Mercy, public domain, available https://commons.wikimedia.org/wiki/File: Divine_Mercy.jpeg

ISBN-13: 979-8-88870-024-2
Library of Congress Control Number: 2022952477

"That you may converse with Jesus face to face and heart to heart."

Peter Arnoudt, SJ
Imitation of the Sacred Heart of Jesus

Table of Contents

Introduction 1

Messages of the Sacred Heart and the Divine

Mercy...5

The Sacred Heart 5

The Divine Mercy 15

St. Margaret Mary Alacoque (1647-1690) 26

St. Faustina Kowalska (1905-1938) 29

Experiences of the Authors......................... 33

The "Rollout" of the Devotions 37

The Sacred Heart Revelations and Devotions...41

First Fridays and the Holy Hour................ 43

Return of Love for Love and the Feast of the

Sacred Heart 46

Image of the Sacred Heart 49

The Divine Mercy Revelations and Devotions 57

The Hour of Great Mercy 58

The Chaplet of Divine Mercy..................... 60

The Novena to Divine Mercy 63

The Image of Divine Mercy 65

The Feast of the Divine Mercy 71

Other Similarities of the Two Devotions 75

The Blessed Virgin Mary 76

Obstacles to Entering Religious Life 79

The Burning of Manuscripts 84

The Promises of the Two Devotions 87

The Sacred Heart Promises 87

The Divine Mercy Promises 90

The Sacred Heart Practices 97

The Divine Mercy Practices 100

Conclusion: How to Blend These Devotions into

Your Life 107

Bibliography 111

Introduction

The purpose of this book is to inspire you to embrace both the Sacred Heart of Jesus and the Divine Mercy of God, by exploring these two devotions and their practices. There is a connection between the heart of Jesus and his love for us, and the mercy of God through which we are redeemed and loved for all eternity. The Sacred Heart of Jesus says something about who God is, and the Divine Mercy says something about what God does.

Jesus's heart is tied to his mercy. His heart refers not only to his physical heart, but also the innermost part of his being, his very love. Devotion to the Sacred Heart of Jesus is an adoring, thankful appreciation of who he is, as Son of the Father and as Redeemer of humankind. Out of this heart flows Divine Mercy, which was the message of the Redemption. "For God so loved the world that he gave his only Son, so that everyone who believes in him may not perish but may have eternal life" (Jn 3:16, *NRSVCE*). This corrects the Fall of Adam and Eve in the Garden of Eden. We can be reconciled to God and eternally united with him by grace through faith (Eph 2:8). This expresses the generous mercy of God by giving each of us a second chance.

Not only that, but creation itself is an act of God's mercy, since there didn't have to be anything created at all. Divine Mercy, then, is God overflowing in love outside of himself, the Trinity expressing Its holy generosity in a magnanimous outpouring of love and creativity. How amazing! We are wanted by the most holy, powerful and loving God, and we are even wanted after the Fall of humankind. Mercy provided for our creation in the first place, and our redemption in the second place, in love through the heart of our Savior.

Devotions to the Sacred Heart of Jesus and the Divine Mercy, as made known through the writings of St. Margaret Mary Alacoque and St. Faustina Kowalska, have many similarities. Both have to do with the heart of Jesus, both were made known through visionaries who were unknown nuns at the time Jesus visited them, both wrote down their visions and had priests who helped them, and both received special instructions from Jesus about the practices that he was inviting people to do and the feasts he wanted established in his honor.

This book aims to show how to embrace the Divine Mercy of God and adore the Most Sacred Heart of Jesus by establishing meaningful connections between the two devotions so that you can practice them happily and grow ever closer to God and experience eternal joy with him forever. May God bless you in the reading of this book!

Messages of the Sacred Heart and the Divine Mercy

The Sacred Heart

"Blessed are the pure in heart,
for they will see God" (Matthew 5:8).

The practice of devotion to the Sacred Heart of Jesus is a mindset, a state of the heart, and a way of life. To enter into the Sacred Heart is a mystical embrace with Jesus. The motivation for practicing this devotion is the desire to pour out our love for God in thanksgiving for what he has done for us, and to console Jesus in a spirit of reparation, of repair, for the outrages and hostility shown against him. We also want to make up for the neglect of him today in the Blessed Sacrament. We visit him in our Churches, we pray to him at home, and we unite our hearts with his.

The heart is the center of a person, the place where love resides. To honor and adore the Sacred Heart of Jesus is to honor him and to love him for himself and for everything he has done for us. It is from his heart that the Church was born, not only in the love Jesus had for the apostles and teaching them how to witness, but also sacramentally, from the blood and water which flowed from his side when his heart was pierced on the cross. Sacramentally, the blood is the Most Precious Blood of Jesus in the sacrament of the Eucharist, and the water signifies the sacrament of Baptism. Therefore we must honor Jesus in his Body and Blood when we take Communion, when we adore the Blessed Sacrament when it is exposed on the altar, and when we recognize Its presence in the tabernacles of all the Churches throughout the world.

Devotion to the Sacred Heart of Jesus developed in the eleventh century, with meditations on the Five Wounds of Christ, although it may be seen as early as the second century with Justin Martyr. Pope Gregory the Great practiced devotion to the Sacred Heart in the seventh century.[1] With St. Bernard and St. Anselm in the twelfth century, there was an increase in devotion to the Sacred Heart. The Franciscan and Dominican friars promoted this devotion, and Saints Gertrude and Mechtild had a special love for the Sacred Heart.[2] The first Feast of the Sacred Heart was celebrated in 1670 in France, by Fr. Jean Eudes.[3]

St. Margaret Mary Alacoque joined the Daughters of the Visitation, founded by St. Francis de Sales and St. Jane Frances de

---

[1] Kathy Schiffer, "Where Did Devotion to the Sacred Heart of Jesus Come From?," at National Catholic Register (19 June 2020), at www.ncregister.com.

[2] Sisters of Reparation to the Most Sacred Heart of Jesus, "History of Devotion to the Sacred Heart of Jesus," at Sacred Heart Basilica, at sacredheartbasilica.com.

[3] Kathy Shiffer, "Where Did Devotion to the Sacred Heart of Jesus Come From?"

Chantal, in 1671. Through Jesus's revelations
to her, and the support of St. Claude de la Colombière, a Jesuit priest who was her spiritual
director, St. Margaret Mary's revelations
were validated and ultimately revealed to
members of her order and the entire Church.
The doctrines contained in her revelations
were further developed and described by
Pope Pius XI in his encyclical *Miserentissi-
mus Redemptor* (1928) and Pope Pius XII in
Haurietis aquas (1956).[4]

Devotion to the Sacred Heart is a matter
of the heart as well as a set of practices. According to Fr. John Croiset, SJ, who was St.
Margaret Mary's spiritual director from
1647-1690,[5] devotion to the Sacred Heart
consists in "ardently loving Jesus Christ,
whom we have always with us in the adorable

---

[4] Sisters of Reparation, "History of Devotion
to the Sacred Heart of Jesus."

[5] John Croiset, SJ, *The Devotion to the Sacred
Heart,* 2nd ed. (Charlotte, NC: Tan Books, 2013),
back cover.

Sacrament of the Eucharist, and in showing this ardent love by our grief at seeing Him so little honored by men, and by our acts of reparation for this contempt and this want of love."[6]

If we are familiar with the story of Jesus's life, from his birth in Bethlehem to his death on the cross, we can sympathize with all of the abuse and shame to which Jesus was exposed during the course of his mortal life. It is not as easy today, perhaps, to recognize the "indignities and outrages" Jesus experiences in the Blessed Sacrament. We do not hear so much today about people abusing the consecrated Host or Precious Blood. Also, many Catholics today may not fully experience or understand the Real Presence of Jesus in our tabernacles, and that it is he, himself who is present on our altars. The practice of the holy hour that the devotion to the Sacred Heart recommends, given by Jesus to St. Margaret

---

[6] Croiset, *Devotion to the Sacred Heart,* 54.

Mary to help make up for the hour that his apostles couldn't stay awake with him in the garden of Gethsemane the night before his crucifixion, can help us patiently pray before the Blessed Sacrament and realize how important Jesus's Real Presence on the altar truly is.

In his encyclical on the Sacred Heart, *Haurietis aquas,* Pope Pius XII described the connection between divine charity and the love and honor every Christian must show in return for the love of Jesus, "Whose wounded Heart is its living token and symbol."[7] He described how charity overflows from "the Heart of the Incarnate Word" into all believers as the members of his Mystical Body, and that this love is so strong that it inspired St. Paul to declare that he is sure that nothing can separate us from the "love of God which is in Christ Jesus our Lord."[8]

---

[7] *Haurietis aquas,* §6.
[8] *Haurietis aquas,* §84.

This love inspires believers to adore Jesus in the Blessed Sacrament, not only as thanksgiving for our redemption but also in response to Jesus's immense love for us, which caused him to shed his blood and give up his life on the cross. Adoration is an act of thankfulness and a return of love for love. This is the motivation for the devotion to the Sacred Heart, and its end is to love Jesus in the Most Blessed Sacrament of the Altar and to provide reparation as a way to console Jesus for the ingratitude of those who may not realize what a precious gift we have received – nothing short of eternal life with God forever in heaven.

A Carthusian from Cologne, Lanspergius (1489-1539), had a deep appreciation for the Sacred Heart and for the wounds of Christ. He described the Sacred Heart as the source of all good:

In Thy Heart I find the beginning of every good thing, the fountain-head of all sweetness and all holy joy. From Thy Heart, O God, Who art goodness itself, proceeds all happiness, sweetness, quietness, joy, peace, gladness, beatitude – in a word, all good gifts . . . Ah! How good it is to draw all that is good from this never failing fountain of the Sacred Heart![9]

Lanspergius connected the love of the heart of Jesus to the wound Jesus suffered in his side:

If thou wouldst touch, in spirit, the Wound of My Side, consider with deep gratitude the love of My Heart, which has led Me to choose thee from all eternity to be My child and the inheritor of my kingdom . . . draw nigh to My Heart which

---

[9] Carthusian Monks, *Ancient Devotions to the Sacred Heart,* 38.

loves thee so much, and has been wounded for thy sake.[10]

In addition to prayer, frequent Communion and visits to the Blessed Sacrament, devotion to the Blessed Virgin Mary is helpful to develop devotion to the Sacred Heart of Jesus. Fr. Croiset recommended that we have "a tender love for the Blessed Virgin who has such absolute power over the Sacred Heart of her Divine Son."[11] He further explained how we should address ourselves to the Blessed Virgin, and how closely her heart is aligned with the Heart of Jesus:

There is no doubt but that the Blessed Virgin is, of all creatures, the one who has loved Jesus Christ most, who has been

---

[10] Carthusian Monks of the XIV-XVII Centuries, *Ancient Devotions to the Sacred Heart of Jesus* (Leominster, UK: Gracewing Publishing, 2018), 32.

[11] Croiset, *Devotion to the Sacred Heart,* 153.

most loved by Him, and who desires most ardently that He be perfectly loved. She is the Mother of perfect love, and it is to her that we should address ourselves in order to be inflamed with that love. The Sacred Hearts of Jesus and Mary are too conformable and too closely united to each other to allow us entry into one without having the entry into the other; with this difference, that the Heart of Jesus suffers only souls extremely pure to enter into that Sanctuary, while the Heart of Mary purifies, by means of the graces she obtains, those souls that are not pure, and puts them in a state to be received into the Heart of Jesus.[12]

Pope St. John Paul II had a love for Mary, as seen in his motto, "Totus Tuus" ("Totally Yours," a phrase which signifies giving one-

---

[12] Croiset, *Devotion to the Sacred Heart,* 153-154.

self entirely to Jesus Christ through Mary).[13] He also had a deep appreciation for the Divine Mercy of God, who accepts the most recalcitrant sinners in his merciful love. The love of Mary can help us approach God even if we are not pure, as described by Lanspergius. There is hope, even for me.

The Divine Mercy

"Blessed are the merciful,
for they will receive mercy" (Matthew 5:7).

Devotion to Divine Mercy can be seen throughout Scripture and the lives of the saints. Fr. Robert Stackpole, Director of the John Paul II Institute of Divine Mercy in Stockbridge, Massachusetts, described Divine Mercy as "God's love reaching down to meet the needs and overcome the miseries of

---

[13] Diocese of Wichita, Kansas, "Overview of Totus Tuus," at totustuus.church, accessed 12/25/22.

His creatures."[14] In the Old Testament, two words were predominantly used for mercy: *hesed* (dependability and steadfastness) and *rachamim* (tenderness and compassion).[15] In the New Testament, the Gospels and the letters reflect Divine Mercy in different ways: "The Gospels show us God's mercy expressed in decisive acts for our salvation ... [and] the Apostolic letters in the New Testament are the praise and proclamation of that mercy, and an exhortation to practice it."[16] Devotion to the Divine Mercy was practiced by many saints, including St. Augustine, St. Bernard, St. Catherine of Siena and St. Therese of Lisieux.[17]

According to the Sisters of Reparation to the Most Sacred Heart of Jesus, devotion to

---

[14] Robert Stackpole, STD, *Divine Mercy: A Guide from Genesis to Benedict XVI* (Stockbridge, MA: Marian Press, 2015), 19.

[15] Stackpole, *Divine Mercy,* 22.

[16] Stackpole, *Divine Mercy,* 71.

[17] Stackpole, *Divine Mercy,* 79-208.

Divine Mercy is a continuation of devotion to the Sacred Heart:

> The Devotion to the Divine Mercy, given to St. Faustina Kowalska in 1931, is a broadened devotion to the Sacred Heart. From this devotion, our trust in God's limitless love and mercy is rekindled. The incomprehensible treasures which we have in the sacraments are symbolized in the blood and water gushing forth from the Heart of Christ. The devotion to the Sacred Heart has flowered and has seemed to come full circle in the devotion to the Divine Mercy, particularly in its emphasis on the graces flowing from the Heart of Jesus, healing and forgiving souls, through the Sacraments of Mercy.[18]

According to Fr. Chris Alar, Director of the Association of Marian Helpers and the head of Marian Press at the National Shrine

---

[18] Sisters of Reparation, "History of Devotion to the Sacred Heart of Jesus."

of The Divine Mercy in Stockbridge, Massachusetts, "Divine Mercy is both a message and a devotion."[19] The message is about God's mercy, and the devotion consists of practices performed by the faithful which reflect the message of mercy. The message of Divine Mercy describes God's three "great acts of mercy."[20] The first act of mercy was creation, the second act of mercy was redemption, and the third act of mercy was sanctification. Creation originated from God's outpouring of love, to generate the universe, plants, trees, animals and people. Redemption, the second act of Divine Mercy, occurred when the Father sent Jesus, his Son, the second Person of the Most Holy Trinity, to be born as a man, die for our sins, and make a way for us to enter heaven. This was extremely merciful, not only in the suffering Jesus endured for us to pay for our sins, but

---

[19] Chris Alar, MIC, *Understanding Divine Mercy* (Stockbridge, MA: Marian Press, 2021), 26.

[20] Alar, *Understanding Divine Mercy*, 17-18.

also in the humanity he assumed to provide for us to be partakers of the divine nature (2 Pet 1:4). Sanctification, the third act of Divine Mercy, was God's gift of grace to provide a way for us to grow in holiness and be with God forever in heaven.

The creation story is found in the book of Genesis. The world and everything in it were created on the first five days, and on the sixth day God created human beings (Gen 1:26-27). Adam and Eve were blessed by God with all good things to eat and everything they would need, even work. They were to "till and keep" the Garden of Eden (Gen 2:15). This gave them something constructive to do.

But something changed. Eve was drawn into a conversation with someone who was not good for her. She engaged a snake. This evil being encouraged her to mistrust God and eat the fruit of the tree of the knowledge of good and evil, of which God had forbidden them to eat. God had even told Adam and Eve that they would die if they ate it (Gen 3:1-3)! The consequences were serious.

The snake was very convincing. Somehow, after talking to this snake, Eve became convinced that the tree was "good for food . . . a delight to the eyes, and . . . desired to make one wise," and she ate it. Adam also ate it (Gen 3:4-7). This singular event is known as The Fall of humankind. It is disastrous. Adam and Eve did die, eventually, and human beings ever since have had a propensity to sin, which leads to misery and death. In fact, the Bible says that the wages of sin is death (Rom 6:23).

Adam and Eve were separated from God. God tried to help them by making clothes out of animal skins for them, which involved the shedding of blood of the very animals he had created. Adam and Eve were banned from the Garden of Eden so that they would not eat from the tree of life and be kept permanently in the fallen state. This was actually merciful because God had a way to redeem humankind, but it would take centuries to put into practice.

God's second act of mercy came to the rescue: this is the Redemption. I like Fra Angelico's painting of the Annunciation, because it shows God's act of initiating the Redemption occurring at the very moment of the Fall. The left side of the painting shows Adam and Eve, ghostlike, covering themselves up in shame after their serious sin.

Annunciation, Fra Angelico, ca. 1435[21]

---

[21] *Annunciation* (Fra Angelico, Madrid) at https://en.wikipedia.org/wiki/Annunciation_ (Fra_Angelico,_Madrid).

The glorious light coming above the angel to Mary takes center stage. But that shaft of light – in shiny gold leaf in the original painting – comes from the very left side of the painting, from a dove in the upper left corner, as though sent from the very moment of the Fall.

When I walked around the corner in the Prado museum in Madrid, into the room where I had come to see this painting, the theological significance of this moment hit me at once. It was a teaching piece. That gold shaft meant that God put his redemptive plan in place from the very beginning of the Fall. There are smaller mini-paintings around the edge of this painting to tell viewers the story of what happened.

Now that we have been freed from sin by the grace of God, through faith (Eph 2:8-9), we can embrace the third act of Divine Mercy, sanctification. Isn't this good news? This is God's third act of mercy, sanctification. We can become "participants of the divine nature" (2 Pet 1:4). The Holy Spirit "came to sanctify us and make us holy so we could return to God the Father without stain or blemish."[22] St. Paul stated that the wages of sin is death, but the free gift of God is eternal life in Christ Jesus our Lord. (Rom 6:22-23). Thanks to the outpouring of grace through the sacraments and teachings of the Church, and to prayer, reading, study, Christian friends and support, we have the means to grow holier and closer to God spiritually and be united with him in his very being.

It amazes me that God embraces you and me, sort of like Mary embraced Jesus. Jesus took on Mary's human nature and was enveloped by her in the womb, so that he could become part of her family. Likewise, God envelops you and me in his grace to allow us to grow in holiness to become part of his family. Indeed, Jesus's very humanity was required by the Redemption to correct the Fall and

---

[22] Alar, *Understanding Divine Mercy,* 18.

allow grace to bring you and me to God. The change that occurred in Jesus's nature made the way for the change that is happening in our nature, through grace.

Through these three acts of Divine Mercy – creation, redemption and sanctification – God has provided for our existence, our return to him even as sinners, and our growth in love and holiness, even to the point of participating in God's own divine nature. Mercy is *misericordia* in Latin, which means "misery" and "heart." Fr. Seraphim Michalenko, MIC, said that this means love (the heart) reaching out to you when you're in misery.[23] All three acts of Divine Mercy – creation, redemption and sanctification – are acts of God's love, reaching out to us and providing mercy and an intimate connection with God which leads to thankfulness and appreciation on our parts.

---

[23] "Daily Minutes with Fr. Seraphim Michalenko, MIC," at https://www.youtube.com/c/DivineMercy_Official.

Development of the Devotions

There are many similarities between the devotions to the Sacred Heart and the Divine Mercy. Both devotions were made known by Jesus through humble nuns, both of whom were asked to write about their mystical encounters with Jesus. Both nuns had priests who supported them and helped to spread the devotions. Both nuns, sadly, became ill early in life and died relatively young. Although they entered different religious orders in different countries and lived in different centuries, in both accounts the importance of obedience to religious superiors was emphasized in their writings and in their lives.

Religious practices to honor Jesus were developed for both devotions, with specific instructions from Jesus regarding the times of day and the purposes of the practices. Both nuns encountered resistance from their families when they chose to enter religious life. Both nuns were canonized as saints. In both cases, new annual feasts were established and attended by Catholics throughout the world, and new daily, weekly and monthly devotional practices were established and grew in popularity, in addition to the annual feasts. The two devotions together have added greatly to our opportunities to draw closer to Jesus in profound faith and love.

St. Margaret Mary Alacoque (1647-1690)

St. Margaret Mary Alacoque was a nun in the Convent of the Visitation at Paray-le-Monial, in Burgundy, France.[24] In her family, she was the fifth of seven children. At age four, she made a vow of chastity to Jesus, and she was devoted from an early age to the Blessed Sacrament and the Blessed Virgin Mary. At the death of her father (age eight), she and her mother were "subjected to domestic persecution and captivity in their own home by some

---

[24] Croiset, *Devotion to the Sacred Heart*, 1.

of their relatives." Margaret took her first Communion at the age of nine.[25]

As a young child, Margaret had rheumatic fever and was in bed for four years. After she made a vow to the Blessed Virgin Mary that she would enter religious life if she were cured, she returned to health. To honor Mary as a result of her healing, she added "Mary" to her name.[26] Margaret's mother and brother were against her choice to enter religious life, and her mother tried to arrange for her to get married. One night, after attending a ball in an evening dress, Margaret had a vision of Christ. He accused her of forgetting about him and "showed her that His heart was full of love for her because of the promise

---

[25] Clarence A. Herbst, SJ, introduction to *The Letters of St. Margaret Mary Alacoque* (Charlotte, NC: Tan Books, 2012), vii-viii.

[26] "Saint Margaret Mary Alacoque," at Catholic Online, at https://www.catholic.org.

she made to his Blessed Mother as a child."[27]
After this vision she was determined to enter
religious life.

Margaret Mary visited the Visitation
nuns at Paray le Monial, France, on May 25,
1671, and she took the habit on August 25,
1671. She made her profession on November
6, 1672. During the period from 1673-1675,
the Lord made around 40 revelations to Sister
Margaret Mary.[28] During these encounters
Jesus revealed to her his Sacred Heart and his
love for all humanity, as well as establishing
various devotional practices to honor his Sacred Heart, including the Feast of the Sacred
Heart, the Holy Hour in remembrance of Jesus's night in Gethsemane, and receiving
Communion on the first Friday of each
month.[29]

---

[27] "Saint Margaret Mary Alacoque," at Catholic Online.

[28] Herbst, introduction to *Letters,* viii-ix.

[29] "Saint Margaret Mary Alacoque," at Catholic Online.

In 1675, Fr. Claude de la Colombière, SJ, was sent to Paray and became Sister Margaret Mary's confessor and spiritual director. He assured her that her revelations were authentic, and he was instrumental in promoting the devotional practices of the Sacred Heart. Despite the resistance and skepticism of some of her religious sisters, Sister Margaret Mary gained their respect over time, and in 1683 she became assistant to the Superior. She was Mistress of Novices from 1685-1686.[30]

Margaret Mary died on October 17, 1690, at the age of 43. Her process of canonization began in 1715. She was declared Venerable in 1824, Blessed in 1864, and she was canonized on May 13, 1920.[31]

St. Faustina Kowalska (1905-1938)

Helena Kowalska, the future St. Faustina, was born to a poor family on a small, rural

---

[30] Herbst, introduction to *Letters,* viii-ix.

[31] Herbst, introduction to *Letters,* viii-ix.

farm in Poland on August 25, 1905. She experienced her first call to religious life at age seven, during adoration. She lived at home but continued to have mystical experiences and "already had a deep, spiritual understanding of the Mass."[32]

In 1924, when Helena was 19, she went to a dance with her sister Natalia and had a vision of Jesus suffering. Jesus asked, "How long shall I put up with you and how long will you keep putting me off?"[33] She went to a nearby cathedral and was told by Jesus to go to Warsaw and join a convent there. After visiting several convents, she was given a chance to join the Sisters of Our Lady of Mercy. She worked for one year to earn enough money to enter the convent, and she received the habit there in April, 1926.

---

[32] Alar, *Understanding Divine Mercy*, 43.

[33] Maria Faustina Kowalska, *Diary: Divine Mercy in My Soul*, 3rd ed. (Stockbridge MA: Marian Press, 2020), no. 9.

In religious life Helena was given the name Maria Faustina of the Blessed Sacrament. She worked as a cook, gardener and portress. She lived in eight different convents in Poland and Lithuania. On February 22, 1931, in Plock, Poland, Jesus appeared to her as the King of Divine Mercy, as pictured in the image of Divine Mercy which she later had painted by an artist.[34]

Sister Maria Faustina arrived in Vilnius on May 25, 1933. Soon afterward, she met Reverend Michael Sopocko who became her spiritual director and promoted devotion to the Divine Mercy.[35] In 1934, Sister Faustina met the artist Eugene Kazimirowski, and she asked him to paint the image of Divine Mercy known as the "Vilnius" image. She worked with him on many revisions until the image

---

[34] Alar, *Understanding Divine Mercy,* 43-45.

[35] Sophia Michalenko, CMGT, *The Life of Faustina Kowalska* (Cincinnati, OH: Franciscan Media, 1999), 68-69.

more closely represented what she had seen in her vision of Jesus.

Sister Faustina continued to receive revelations from Jesus and she wrote down her experiences in a diary that she was asked to write by Jesus himself, and by Fr. Sopocko and Fr. Andrasz.[36] She worked closely with her spiritual director, Fr. Sopocko, to establish and promote devotion to the Divine Mercy. She became ill with tuberculosis and died on October 5, 1938. She was canonized by Pope St. John Paul II on April 30, 2000. Pope St. John Paul II made it a large part of his life's work to promote devotion to the Divine Mercy, culminating in the canonization of St. Faustina and the official designation of the Sunday after Easter as Divine Mercy Sunday. His encyclical on the Divine Mercy, *Dives in misericordia,* was published on November 30, 1980.

---

[36] Congregation of the Sisters of Our Lady of Mercy, "Diary," at saint-faustina.org.

Experiences of the Authors

Both St. Margaret Mary Alacoque and St. Faustina Kowalska experienced mystical revelations from Jesus. He spoke to them about what to write, the purpose and message of the revelations, and how the devotions would be spread. Both saints were asked by their spiritual directors to record their revelations in writing, and Jesus supported the nuns' obedience to their superiors.

The accounts of the revelations reveal similarities in how the two saints experienced their encounters with Jesus. Both St. Margaret Mary and St. Faustina experienced visions of Jesus after a dance, asking them why they were keeping him waiting to enter religious life. Both received instructions about their writing and creating images of Jesus. Both authors recorded practical devotions given by Jesus to help the faithful build their love of him and increase their faith. In both cases Jesus provided instructions about feasts to be established in the Church, and both feasts were tied to existing feasts (Corpus Christi and Easter) and would follow them in the liturgical calendar of the Church.

In St. Faustina's *Diary* there are references both to the Sacred Heart of Jesus and to the Divine Mercy. Since mercy flows from the heart of Jesus, it makes sense that the two devotions are interrelated. In one experience at Mass, St. Faustina described not only the Lord's mercy but also his Sacred Heart:

> I felt that I had been completely immersed in Him. During Holy Mass, my love for Him reached a peak of intensity. After the renewal of vows and Holy Communion, I suddenly saw the Lord Jesus, who said to me with great kindness, 'My daughter, look at my merciful Heart.' As I fixed my gaze on the Most Sacred Heart, the same rays of light, as are represented in the image as blood and water, came

forth from it, and I understood how great is the Lord's mercy.[37]

St. Faustina had experiences which showed a deep intimacy with the Sacred Heart. She recorded that she practiced the holy hour of adoration, which is associated with devotion to the Sacred Heart of Jesus.[38] Jesus also referred to St. Faustina's heart, calling it his heaven ("My daughter, your heart is My heaven").[39] During Mass on the day of her perpetual vows, St. Faustina placed her heart "on the paten where Your heart has been placed," to offer herself, with Jesus, to God. She prayed, "Father of Mercy, look upon the sacrifice of my heart, but through the wound in the Heart of Jesus." Jesus affirmed her wish to unite her heart with his when she heard him say, "My spouse, our hearts are joined forever. Remember to Whom you have

---

[37] Kowalska, *Diary,* no. 177.

[38] Kowalska, *Diary,* no. 237.

[39] Kowalska, *Diary,* no. 238.

vowed." Shortly after this she prayed, "Jesus I trust in You! Jesus I love You with all my heart!"[40]

It was the heart of Jesus that was pierced on the cross, out of which flowed blood and water. This very blood which paid the price for our sins is now present in the Eucharist, which is the source and summit of our sacramental life as Catholics. Jesus showed us how important the Eucharist would become by sharing the Last Supper with his disciples. Today in the Eucharist we encounter the Body, Blood, Soul and Divinity of Jesus Christ, as we say in the Divine Mercy Chaplet.

Jesus's strong and loving relationship with St. Faustina were especially touching in her *Diary* entries at the time of her perpetual vows in 1933. The day before she took her vows, she heard Jesus say, "'My daughter,

---

[40] Kowalska, *Diary*, no. 239.

your heart is My heaven,'"[41] On the day of her vows (May 1, 1933), she wrote, "Jesus, from now on Your Heart is mine, and mine is Yours alone," and during the vows she heard Jesus say to her, "'My spouse, our hearts are joined forever. Remember to Whom you have vowed." She wrote, "Jesus, I trust in You! . . . I die completely to myself today and begin to live for the greater glory of Your Holy Name."[42]

The "Rollout" of the Devotions

Both devotions were implemented or "rolled out" with key elements that were similar:

- Leadership and Purpose: Both devotions had the strong leadership of Jesus himself as he revealed his plans to

---

[41] Kowalska, *Diary,* no. 238.

[42] Kowalska, *Diary,* no. 239.

two devoted nuns. The purpose of
each devotion was to foster a return to
faith in Jesus and his merciful love.

- <u>Governance and Usefulness</u>: Both devotions provided written accounts to
  guide the faithful to greater devotion
  and to allow for consistency in their
  practices. This made the devotions
  useful for a wide variety of people in
  many different settings.

- <u>Attitudes, Feelings and Resistance</u>:
  The two nuns encountered resistance
  from their relatives, and at times from
  members of their own communities,
  as they promoted the new devotions.
  Gradually, people's attitudes changed
  as they saw the sincerity of the nuns
  as they learned more about their revelations, and observed how the priests
  who helped them validated the authenticity of their accounts.

- **Social Support:** Both nuns had the support of priests who carefully examined and listened to accounts of their encounters with Jesus and validated their authenticity and consistency with Church teachings. Although social support was limited at first, each nun gained the support of her superiors and others in their communities over time.

For more on the elements of change during the implementation of any innovation, particularly those in Catholic religious orders, see *Principles of Change: Teresa of Avila's Carmelite Reform and Insights from Change Management*.[43]

---

[43] Kristina Olsen, PhD, DBA, *Principles of Change: Teresa of Avila's Carmelite Reform and Insights from Change Management* (St. Louis: En Route Books and Media, 2022).

The Sacred Heart Revelations and Devotions

Jesus explained to St. Margaret Mary that he had chosen her to accomplish the spread of the devotion to his Sacred Heart:

My Divine Heart . . . is so inflamed with love for men, and for thee in particular that, being unable any longer to contain within Itself the flames of Its burning Charity, It must needs spread them abroad by thy means, and manifest Itself to them (mankind) in order to enrich them with the precious treasures which I discover to thee, and which contain graces of sanctification and salvation necessary to withdraw them from the abyss of perdition. I have chosen thee as an abyss of unworthiness and ignorance for the accomplishment of this great design.[44]

After saying this, Jesus asked Margaret Mary for her heart, which she gave him, and he "placed it in His own Adorable Heart where He showed it to me as a little atom which was being consumed in this great furnace." He then returned it to her as "a burning flame in the form of a heart . . . as a precious token of My love," and gave her the title of "'beloved disciple of My Sacred Heart.'" However, this event caused a wound in her side which was healed by Jesus, but which would always cause her pain. This event was "'the foundation of all those which I intend further to confer upon thee,'" Jesus told her.[45]

---

[44] Margaret Mary Alacoque, *The Autobiography of Saint Margaret Mary*, trans. Sisters of the Visitation, Kent, England (Charlotte, NC: Tan Books, 2012), 53.

[45] Alacoque, *Autobiography,* 53-55.

First Fridays and the Holy Hour

It was only after a number of revelations to St. Margaret Mary that Jesus began to show her the meaning and importance of various practices that would come to be associated with the Sacred Heart. On the first Friday of each month, St. Margaret Mary received a renewal of the revelation she received above, which she called "the grace connected with the pain in my side." On one occasion, she received a vision of Jesus's Sacred Heart as a profound image:

> The Sacred Heart was represented to me as a resplendent sun, the burning rays of which fell vertically upon my heart, which was inflamed with a fire so fervid that it seemed as if it would reduce me to ashes . . . Jesus Christ, my sweet Master, presented Himself to me, all resplendent

with glory, His Five Wounds shining like
so many suns.[46]

After this Jesus described how much he
had loved men, "from whom He received
only ingratitude and contempt." He then told
St. Margaret Mary, "'Do thou at least console
me by supplying for their ingratitude, as far
as thou art able.'"[47] She wasn't sure how she
could accomplish this.

Jesus told her:

In the first place thou shalt receive Me in
Holy Communion as often as obedience
will permit thee . . . Thou shalt, moreover,
communicate on the First Friday of each
month. Every night between Thursday
and Friday I will make thee share in the
mortal sadness which I was pleased to feel

[46] Alacoque, *Autobiography,* 55-56.
[47] Alacoque, *Autobiography,* 56.

in the Garden of Olives . . . And in order to bear Me company in the humble prayer that I then offered to My Father in the midst of My anguish, thou shalt rise between eleven o'clock and midnight, and remain prostrate with Me for an hour, not only to appease the divine anger by begging mercy for sinners, but also to mitigate in some way the bitterness which I felt at that time on finding Myself abandoned by My apostles, which obliged Me to reproach them for not being able to watch one hour with Me.[48]

From these descriptions of St. Margaret Mary's encounters with Jesus, we see the Sacred Heart of Jesus revealed to her, as well as the admonition to receive Holy Communion on the first Friday of each month, and to spend an hour in prayer with Jesus as a way

---

[48] Margaret Mary Alacoque, *Autobiography*, 57.

of praying for sinners and mitigating Jesus's pain of abandonment which he felt during his prayer in the Garden of Gethsemane.

Return of Love for Love and the Feast of the Sacred Heart

One time, when St. Margaret Mary was in prayer before the Blessed Sacrament during the eight days following the feast of Corpus Christi, she "received from my God signal tokens of His love, and felt urged with the desire of making Him some return, and of rendering Him love for love."

Jesus responded that she should continue to do what he had asked her to do, and he shared his sadness at having been rejected by so many people:

Thou canst not make me a greater return of love . . . than by doing what I have so often asked of thee." Then, discovering to me His Divine Heart, He said: "Behold this Heart, which has loved men so much, that It has spared nothing . . . in order to testify to them Its love; and in return I receive from the greater number nothing but ingratitude by reason of their irreverence and sacrileges, and by the coldness and contempt which they show Me in this Sacrament of Love."[49]

Jesus then asked St. Margaret Mary to establish the Feast of the Sacred Heart:

Therefore, I ask of thee that the Friday after the Octave of Corpus Christi be set apart for a special Feast to honor my Heart, by communicating on that day and making reparation to It by a solemn act, in order to make amends for the indignities which It has received during the time It has been exposed on the altars.[50]

---

[49] Alacoque, *Autobiography,* 95.
[50] Alacoque, *Autobiography,* 95-96.

Fr. Croiset described the relationship of the Feast of Corpus Christi to the Feast of the Sacred Heart as the love of Jesus for us in giving us his Body and Blood (Corpus Christi), and the love we return in thanks to him for all he has done for us (Sacred Heart):

Our amiable Saviour has Himself chosen the Friday after the octave as a second special feast on which His Sacred Heart may be truly adored by perfect friends. The first feast referred to is the feast of Corpus Christi, the second is the feast of His Sacred Heart. The love which He has for us triumphs in the first; the love which we have for Him ought to triumph in the second. In the first feast, the Church shows in a solemn manner to what extreme Jesus Christ loves us; in the second, we should protest in the face of Heaven and earth how sincerely we love Jesus Christ.[51]

Jesus promised that his heart would "shed in abundance the influence of Its divine love upon those who shall thus honor It, and cause It to be honored."[52] When St. Margaret Mary replied that she did not know how she would accomplish this, Jesus told her to speak to the priest he had sent to work with her, who was Fr. Claude de la Colombière. Fr. de la Colombière asked St. Margaret Mary to write down her experiences of Jesus and his Sacred Heart, and he reassured her that her revelations were genuine.

Image of the Sacred Heart

The well-known image of the Sacred Heart as a heart encircled with thorns, burn-

---

[51] Croiset, *Devotion to the Sacred Heart,* 172-173.

[52] Alacoque, *Autobiography,* 96.

ing with flames with a cross above it, was described in two letters written by St. Margaret
Mary in 1689, one to Mother de Saumaise at
Dijón, and the other to Fr. Croiset. In the first
letter, written in January of 1689, St. Margaret Mary described an experience she had on
the Feast of St. John the Evangelist (probably
December 27, 1688):

> I had the incomparable happiness, to-
> gether with that beloved disciple, of rest-
> ing on the breast of this divine Spouse, of
> Whom I am so unworthy, and that He
> gave me His Heart, His cross, and His
> love. He gave me His Heart to be my ref-
> uge, my help in all my needs, and my ha-
> ven of repose amidst the storms and tem-
> pests on this sea of life. There the cross
> must be my throne of glory. On it alone
> must I find my joy. Nothing means any-
> thing to me any more but Jesus, His love,
> and the cross – most of all His holy love,

to purify me, consume me, and transform me into Him.[53]

In a second letter written to Fr. Croiset on November 3, 1689, St. Margaret Mary described the image of the Sacred Heart more clearly. She had just been writing about how Jesus had complete control over her and was the "Sovereign of my soul":

> But to return to what you want to know touching the Sacred Heart. The first special grace I think I received in this regard was on the feast of Saint John the Evangelist. Our Lord made me rest for several hours on His sacred breast and from this lovable Heart I received graces whose very memory carries me out of myself . . .

---

[53] Margaret Mary Alacoque, *The Letters of St. Margaret Mary Alacoque,* trans. Clarence A. Herbst (Charlotte, NC: Tan Books, 2012), 139.

I saw this divine Heart as on a throne of
flames, more brilliant than the sun and
transparent as crystal. It had Its adorable
wound and was encircled with a crown of
thorns, which signified the pricks our sins
caused Him. It was surmounted by a
cross which signified that, from the first
moment of His Incarnation, that is, from
the time this Sacred Heart was formed,
the cross was planted in It; that It was
filled, from the very first moment, with all
the bitterness, humiliations, poverty, sor-
row, and contempt His sacred humanity
would have to suffer during the whole
course of His life and during His holy
Passion.[54]

St. Margaret Mary continued by weaving
together themes of "love, mercy, grace, sanctification and salvation":

---

[54] Alacoque, *Letters,* 229-230

He made me understand that the ardent desire He had of being loved by men and of drawing them from the path of perdition . . . had caused Him to fix upon this plan of manifesting His Heart to men, together with all Its treasures of love, mercy, grace, sanctification and salvation. This He did in order that those who were willing to do all in their power to render and procure for Him honor, love, and glory might be enriched abundantly, even profusely, with these divine treasures of the Heart of God, which is their source. It must be honored under the symbol of this Heart of flesh, Whose image he wished to be publicly exposed . . . Wherever this sacred image would be exposed for veneration He would pour forth His graces and blessings. This devotion was as a last effort of His love which wished to favor men in these last centuries with this loving redemption, in order to withdraw them from the empire of Satan, which He intended to destroy, and in order to put us under the sweet liberty of the empire of His love. This He would establish in the hearts of all those who would embrace this devotion.[55]

Sacred Heart of Jesus [56]

St. Margaret Mary recorded one event concerning the image of the Sacred Heart, that occurred when she was Mistress of

---

[55] Alacoque, *Letters,* 229-230

[56] Holy card of the author.

Novices. On the feast of St. Margaret, she asked the novices to honor the Sacred Heart of Jesus rather than give her the "little marks of honor" which were intended for her. The feast fell on a Friday that year. They agreed and make a "little altar whereupon they placed a small ink etching representing the Divine Heart." They honored this image of the Sacred Heart. Later they were criticized for wanting to start a new devotion, and St. Margaret Mary was "forbidden henceforth to put any picture of the Sacred Heart in a conspicuous place, being allowed merely to honor It in private."[57] This was a cause of affliction for her, so she took it to Jesus in prayer. He reassured her, saying, "Fear nothing. I shall reign in spite of My enemies." She was consoled and "abandoned to Him the defence of His own cause while I suffered in silence." She viewed the persecutions she experienced as an opportunity to participate in

---

[57] Alacoque, *Autobiography*, 97.

"the share He gave me of His Cross, a most delicious viand of which I never grew weary."[58]

Representations of the Sacred Heart developed over time. Images of the Sacred Heart from the time of St. Margaret Mary were in graphic detail, including blood dripping from the heart. More recently, Jesus is pictured as looking directly at the viewer with a stylized representation of His heart encircled by a crown of thorns, with a cross above it and flames around it. Today, the veneration of the image of the Sacred Heart, the Holy Hour of Reparation, the practice of taking Communion on First Fridays and the Feast of the Sacred Heart have come to be important aspects of Catholic devotion that have spread throughout the world from the revelations of Jesus and his love to St. Margaret Mary at Paray-le-Monial, France, in the 17th century.

---

[58] Alacoque, *Autobiography*, 98.

The Divine Mercy
Revelations and Devotions

The foundations of the devotional practices to the Divine Mercy are rooted in the life of Jesus, especially his Passion. Three o'clock p.m. is the Hour of Great Mercy associated with the time he died on the cross on Good Friday. The Chaplet of Divine Mercy is to be recited at this hour if possible, and the Novena of chaplets invites specific groups of people to come to Jesus to be healed. The image of Jesus with the statement, "Jesus I Trust In You," conveys Jesus's merciful love and welcoming invitation to come to him for mercy, and the red and pale rays emanating from the heart of Jesus represent the water and blood that flowed from the wound in his side when he was pierced by a lance after his death. The Feast of Divine Mercy, celebrated on the Sunday after Easter, serves as a completion of the Easter message and the fulfillment of the Redemption wrought by Jesus for all humankind. During this Feast we can freely come to him for forgiveness, love and mercy. The specifics of these devotional practices are discussed below.

The revelations of Jesus to St. Faustina were recorded in her *Diary.*[59] In it, Jesus described to St. Faustina the practices he wanted to introduce to the faithful, in order to share with them an understanding of his profound and endless mercy toward all people, and to inspire them to come to him for forgiveness, mercy and love.

The Hour of Great Mercy

St. Faustina recorded Jesus's words to her about the Hour of Great Mercy between 3:00 and 4:00 p.m., and he advised her what to do at this time each day:

---

[59] Maria Faustina Kowalska, *Diary: Divine Mercy in My Soul,* 3rd ed. (Stockbridge MA: Marian Press, 2020).

I remind you, My daughter, that as often as you hear the clock strike the third hour, immerse yourself completely in My mercy, adoring and glorifying it; invoke its omnipotence for the whole world, and particularly for poor sinners; for at that moment mercy was opened wide for every soul. In this hour you can obtain everything for yourself and for others for the asking; it was the hour of grace for the whole world – mercy triumphed over justice.[60]

Jesus went on to ask St. Faustina to try her best to make the Stations of the Cross or at least step into the chapel and "'adore, in the Blessed Sacrament, My Heart, which is full of mercy.'" If she couldn't step into the chapel, she could pray for a moment wherever she happened to be.[61]

---

[60] Kowalska, *Diary,* no. 1572.

[61] Kowalska, *Diary,* no. 1572.

Three o'clock in the afternoon is a good time to pray. In the middle of the afternoon I'm often tired and sometimes frustrated by how the day has gone and what I have not yet been able to accomplish. At this time, if I can pray even part of the chaplet, however briefly, I am comforted and reminded how much Jesus loves me, and you, too.

The Chaplet of Divine Mercy

Jesus asked St. Faustina to pray specific prayers, and he gave her the words to use. For example, in *Diary* entries 186-187, Jesus recalled his Passion and tied this to the love of his Heart:

> I desire that you know more profoundly the love that burns in My Heart for souls, and you will understand this when you meditate upon My Passion. Call upon My mercy on behalf of sinners; I desire their salvation. When you say this prayer, with

a contrite heart and with faith on behalf of some sinner, I will give him the grace of conversion.

This is the prayer: "O Blood and Water, which gushed forth from the Heart of Jesus as a found of Mercy for us, I trust in you."[62]

This prayer is recited at the beginning of the Chaplet of Divine Mercy. Another prayer associated with the Chaplet was prayed by St. Faustina as a way to intercede for a town in Poland.[63] When she saw an angel "clothed in a dazzling robe, his face gloriously bright, a cloud beneath his feet," ready to strike the place on earth (which she does not name) as a chastisement for their sins, she implored the Angel to "hold off for a few moments, and the world would do penance." She felt the power of Jesus's grace in her soul and "was instantly

---

[62] Kowalska, *Diary,* no. 186-187.

[63] Alar, *Understanding Divine Mercy,* 110.

snatched up before the Throne of God. Oh, how great is our Lord and God and how incomprehensible his holiness!" St. Faustina prayed as follows: "Eternal Father, I offer You the Body and Blood, Soul and Divinity of Your dearly beloved Son, Our Lord Jesus Christ for our sins and those of the whole world; for the sake of His sorrowful Passion, have mercy on us."[64]

The next morning, when she entered the chapel, she was given the rest of the Chaplet. She was told by Jesus to pray the prayer from the day before (quoted above) every time she entered the chapel, and that "this prayer will serve to appease My wrath. You will recite it for nine days, on the beads of the rosary, in the following manner":

First of all, you will say one OUR FA-THER and HAIL MARY and the I BE-LIEVE IN GOD. Then on the OUR

---

[64] Kowalska, *Diary,* no. 474-475.

FATHER beads you will say the following words: "Eternal Father, I offer You the Body and Blood, Soul and Divinity of Your dearly beloved Son, Our Lord Jesus Christ, in atonement for our sins and those of the whole world." On the HAIL MARY beads you will say the following words: "For the sake of His sorrowful Passion have mercy on us and on the whole world." In conclusion, three times you will recite these words: "Holy God, Holy Might One, Holy Immortal One, have mercy on us and on the whole world." [65]

The Novena to Divine Mercy

In one revelation, Jesus told St. Faustina to write down the Novena to Divine Mercy, which would consist of a Chaplet of Divine Mercy on each of nine days beginning on

---

[65] Kowalska, *Diary,* no. 476.

Good Friday. On each of the nine days, the Chaplet would be offered for specific groups of people, to pray for mercy for them. Jesus instructed St. Faustina to bring these souls to him so that they would find the strength and grace they needed for whatever situation they were in, as well as for the hour of their death. Jesus told her that he would bring them to the Father, and that she would continue to bring souls to him even after her death. He would not deny anything to any soul who St. Faustina would bring to him for mercy. She was to ask the Father for graces for them, based on his Passion.[66]

The groups of souls that Jesus asked St. Faustina to bring to him were the following: all people, including sinners (Day 1), priests and religious (Day 2), devout and faithful souls (Day 3), pagans and those who did yet know Jesus (Day 4), heretics and schismatics (Day 5), children and humble souls (Day 6),

---

[66] Kowalska, *Diary,* no. 1209.

those who especially venerated his mercy (Day 7), and the souls in Purgatory (Day 9). St. Faustina recorded a special prayer in the *Diary* for each group of souls.[67]

Today, the Novena to Divine Mercy is said daily by the seminarians at the Shrine of Divine Mercy in Stockbridge, Massachusetts. Online viewers may join them each day at 3:00 p.m. for this novena.[68]

The Image of Divine Mercy

On the evening of February 22, 1931, St. Faustina was alone in her room. She had a revelation of Jesus in the way that we now see depicted in the image of the Divine Mercy:

In the evening, when I was in my cell, I saw the Lord Jesus clothed in a white garment. One hand [was] raised in the

---

[67] Kowalska, *Diary*, no. 1210-1229.

[68] See https://www.thedivinemercy.org/DailyChaplet.

gesture of blessing, the other was touching the garment at the breast. From beneath the garment, slightly drawn aside at the breast, there were emanating two large rays, one red, the other pale. In silence I kept my gaze fixed on the Lord; my soul was struck with awe, but also with great joy. After a while, Jesus said to me, "Paint an image according to the pattern you see, with the signature: Jesus I trust in You. I desire that this image be venerated, first in your chapel, and [then] throughout the world."[69]

According to St. Faustina, Jesus then promised that those who would venerate the image would not perish, and that he would defend them over their enemies and at the hour of their death. [70]

---

[69] Kowalska, *Diary,* no. 47.

[70] Kowalska, *Diary,* no. 48.

The guidance St. Faustina received from her confessor was that this exchange referred to the image of Jesus in her soul. When she brought this information to Jesus, he replied that his image was already in her soul. He continued, "I desire that there be a Feast of Mercy. I want this image, which you will paint with a brush, to be solemnly blessed on the first Sunday after Easter; that Sunday is to be the Feast of Mercy."[71] Jesus went on to say that he wanted priests to proclaim his mercy to sinners so that they would feel unafraid to approach him.[72]

In 1934, Fr. Sopocko introduced St. Faustina to a painter, Eugene Kazimirowski. St. Faustina worked with the painter, who repainted the image several times to conform to St. Faustina's wishes.[73] Even though it never quite looked good enough to St. Faustina, Jesus said to her, "Not in the beauty of the

[71] Kowalska, *Diary,* no. 49

[72] Kowalska, *Diary,* no. 50.

[73] Alar, *Understanding Divine Mercy,* 47.

color, nor of the brush lies the greatness of this image, but in my grace."[74] The image painted by Kazimirowski, known as the "Vilnius" image because of the city in which it was painted, was finally finished in June, 1934 and placed in the convent of the Bernardine Sisters near the church of St. Michael, where Fr. Sopocko was the pastor.[75] St. Faustina wrote that under Fr. Sopocko's direction her love of God increased and that many of the Lord's wishes were carried out.[76] A footnote in the *Diary* explained that St. Faustina had in mind the painted image of Christ with the signature, "Jesus I trust in You," along with making known the Chaplet and Novena of Divine Mercy.[77]

The Paschal Mystery – the Passion, death, Resurrection and Ascension of Jesus – is

---

[74] Kowalska, *Diary,* no. 313.

[75] Sophia Michalenko, *The Life of Faustina Kowalska,* 78.

[76] Kowalska, *Diary,* no. 144.

[77] Kowalska, *Diary,* note 46, p. 657.

reflected in the image of Divine Mercy. In the image, Jesus wears the white robe of the Jewish High Priest. Jesus's right hand is raised in blessing, as the High Priest would do when he came out of the Holy of Holies, the inner sanctuary of the Temple. Jesus is the new High Priest, as described in the book of Hebrews. He offered himself as the perfect sacrifice for all humankind, replacing Jewish animal sacrifices, which only temporarily atoned for the sins of the Hebrew people.[78]

Also, Jesus told St. Faustina that the two rays in the image represented blood and water:

The two rays denote Blood and Water. The pale ray stands for the Water which makes souls righteous. The red ray stands for the Blood which is the life of souls . . . These two rays issued forth from the very

---

[78] Alar, *Understanding Divine Mercy*, 94.

"Jesus I trust in You."

Divine Mercy [79]

---

[79] After Adolf Hyla, Painting of the Divine Mercy, Archives of the Congregation of the Sisters of Our Lady of Mercy, public domain, available https://commons.wikimedia.org/wiki/File: Divine_Mercy.jpeg

depths of My tender mercy when My agonized Heart was opened by a lance on
the Cross. These rays shield souls from
the wrath of My Father. Happy is the one
who will dwell in their shelter, for the just
hand of God shall not lay hold of him. I
desire that the first Sunday after Easter be
the Feast of Mercy.[80]

Contemplating the image of Divine
Mercy reminds us that Jesus is always seeking
us out and ready to forgive and bless us. It is
an invitation to be drawn into his merciful,
powerful love.

The Feast of the Divine Mercy

Jesus told St. Faustina about the fathom-
less mercy he wanted to invite people to experience on the Feast of Divine Mercy, the

---

[80] Kowalska, *Diary,* no. 299.

Sunday after Easter. He asked her to tell the whole world about his mercy and he described the Feast of Mercy:

> I desire that the Feast of Mercy be a refuge and shelter for all souls, and especially for poor sinners. On that day the very depths of My tender mercy are open. I pour out a whole ocean of graces upon those souls who approach the Fount of My Mercy. The soul that will go to Confession and receive Holy Communion shall obtain complete forgiveness of sins and punishment.[81]

The image of Jesus was first displayed during the three days leading up to, and including, the second Sunday of Easter (Divine Mercy Sunday), April 26 to 28, 1935. It was placed in the window of a church near the icon of the Blessed Virgin Mary during the

---

[81] Kowalska, *Diary*, no. 699.

celebration for the closing of the Jubilee Year of the Redemption of the World.[82]

The second Sunday of Easter was formally designated as the Sunday of Divine Mercy by Pope St. John Paul II on April 30, 2000, which was the second Sunday of Easter that year. On the same day, Pope St. John Paul II canonized St. Faustina Kowalska. From that time the popularity of Divine Mercy Sunday grew rapidly. Images of the Divine Mercy are often carried in procession on that day and placed in the Church to be venerated by the people who come to worship on that day.[83]

---

[82] Michalenko, *Life of Faustina Kowalska*, 96.

[83] "Divine Mercy Sunday," at en.wikipedia.org.

Other Similarities
of the Two Devotions

The lives and experiences of St. Margaret Mary Alacoque and St. Faustina Kowalska were similar in a number of ways. Both had a special devotion to the Blessed Virgin Mary, who appeared to them and kept them safe. Both had difficulty entering religious life, due to pressure from their relatives. Both saints saw Jesus wounded and disfigured after they had spent a night out with friends, and for both this experience was a powerful way to bring them back to their intentions to enter religious life. Both saints burned early manuscripts of their writings, after which each was ordered to rewrite what had been lost. Both saints understood the importance of obedience to their superiors, and they made great efforts to conform to what was required of them.

The Blessed Virgin Mary

St. Margaret Mary and St. Faustina both had special relationships with the Blessed Virgin Mary. St. Margaret Mary wrote that the Blessed Virgin had always taken great care of her. She wrote that she went to the Blessed Virgin Mary with all her needs, and that Mary preserved her from "great dangers." St. Margaret Mary often said the rosary on her bare knees, or "genuflecting and kissing the ground at every Ave Maria." [84] When she was severely ill for four years as a child, "unable to walk, my bones piercing my skin," she was consecrated to the Blessed Virgin, "with the promise that, if she cured me, I should one day be one of her daughters."[85]

Margaret Mary described her cure and how the Blessed Virgin took her under her protection, in her *Autobiography*:

---

[84] Margaret Mary Alacoque, *Autobiography*, 2.

[85] Alacoque, *Autobiography*, 3-4.

Scarcely had I made this vow, than I was cured and taken anew under the protection of Our Lady. She made herself so completely Mistress of my heart, that, looking upon me as her own, she governed me as wholly dedicated to her, reproving me for my faults and teaching me how to do the Will of God.[86]

When St. Margaret Mary had problems with her brother at the time she wanted to enter religious life, she had Masses said in honor of the Blessed Virgin Mary, who, "to console me, said lovingly: 'Fear nothing, thou shalt be my true daughter, and I will always be thy good Mother.'"[87]

St. Faustina also had a special relationship with Mary, and she reported seeing her and hearing her on several occasions. On August 5, 1935, the Feast of Our Lady of Mercy,

---

[86] Alacoque, *Autobiography,* 4.

[87] Alacoque, *Autobiography,* 31-32.

Faustina had been struggling with the idea that she would have to leave her community to establish a new one. However, while she was praying, the Blessed Virgin Mary appeared to her, held her close, and told her that she was the mother of all of them, thanks to God's mercy. She emphasized that they should faithfully do the will of God. Mary encouraged her to be courageous and to fix her eyes on Jesus's Passion in order to be victorious.[88]

On November 29, 1936, the Blessed Virgin Mary helped St. Faustina prepare for Christmas. Our Lady appeared to St. Faustina and she told her to seek silence and humility so Jesus could rest. Jesus lived in her heart, she said, and she told St. Faustina to adore him there and not go out from her inmost being. Jesus would make known to her how to commune with him.[89]

---

[88] Kowalska, *Diary*, no. 449.
[89] Kowalska, *Diary*, no. 785.

Obstacles to Entering Religious Life

St. Margaret Mary and St. Faustina both encountered obstacles from their families when they decided to enter religious life. St. Margaret Mary received several offers of marriage, and her relatives pressed her to accept an offer of marriage so that her mother would be taken care of and consoled to see that her daughter was settled. In an effort to convince her daughter to marry, St. Margaret Mary's mother told her about "the tears she shed, suggesting that she would die of grief if I became a nun and that, as she depended entirely upon me for the care and attendance she required, I would be responsible for her death before God."[90]

This made St. Margaret Mary cry, too, and caused her to "suffer a martyrdom . . . not knowing what course to take and having no one to whom I could open my heart." But

---

[90] Alacoque, *Autobiography,* 14-15.

"the tender love for my mother began to get the upper hand," and she began to dress up and attend dances, reasoning that she was only a child when she made her promise to the Blessed Virgin Mary to enter religious life after being cured of a major illness.[91]

One night, after coming home and taking off "those accursed liveries of Satan, namely all that worldly attire," Jesus appeared to St. Margaret Mary "torn and disfigured as at the time of His scourging." Jesus said that it was her vanity that had reduced him to that state, and he added that she had "betrayed and persecuted Him, regardless of the many proofs he had given me of His love."[92]

This caused St. Margaret Mary to weep bitterly, and to go through many conflicts before arriving at a final decision to enter religious life. The decision came after more encounters with Jesus. One time Jesus shared

---

[91] Alacoque, *Autobiography,* 15.

[92] Alacoque, *Autobiography,* 16-17.

that he wanted to make of her "a compound
of My Love and of My Mercy," and on another occasion he told her that he had "chosen thee to be my spouse and we pledged each
other fidelity when thou didst make thy vow
of Chastity. It was I Who urged thee to make
it, before the world had any share in thy
heart."[93] He had then given her into the care
of his mother, the Blessed Virgin Mary.

After more struggles and resistance from
her family, St. Margaret Mary finally made a
definite decision to enter religious life. Jesus
came to her saying, "If thou art faithful to Me
and followest Me, I will teach thee to know
Me, and I will manifest Myself to thee," and
he gave her such a strong sense of peace while
she was listening to Him that she "resolved
henceforth to die rather than to change," and
her "bonds were broken." Jesus then re-
quested that he become the "Master of [her]
liberty," if she agreed, which she did, and he

---

[93] Alacoque, *Autobiography,* 22.

"penetrated so gently and deeply into my heart that I renewed my vow." From that time forward St. Margaret Mary dismissed all suitors and had her heart set on entering religious life.[94]

St. Faustina also experienced resistance from her family. When she went to her parents to share her wish to enter a convent, they refused to pay attention to her. Her father said he had no money for a dowry, but St. Faustina said she didn't need any money because "Jesus Himself will lead me to a convent." Her parents still refused to allow her to enter religious life.[95]

St. Faustina became afraid of God's great plans for her, and she questioned her ability to fulfill them. She once heard the words, "You will prepare the world for My final coming."[96] However, she avoided conver-

---

[94] Alacoque, *Autobiography,* 24-25.

[95] Sophia Michalenko, *Life of Faustina Kowalska,* 20-21.

[96] Kowalska, *Diary,* no. 429.

sations with Jesus due to her inner fear and conflicts. She shared this with Fr. Sopocko, and he urged her to listen to the words God was speaking. The next time Jesus appeared to her, he allowed her to rest her head on his chest and he told her to fear nothing.[97] He reminded her that she was his dwelling place, and that for her sake he would bless the earth.[98]

St. Faustina entered religious life in April, 1926, after an experience of seeing Jesus suffer due to her delay. She immediately went to a cathedral to pray, and then to Warsaw where she visited a number of convents. She ultimately entered the Congregation of the Sisters of Our Lady of Mercy in 1926.[99]

---

[97] Michalenko, *Life of Faustina Kowalska,* 100.

[98] Kowalska, *Diary,* no. 431.

[99] Alar, *Understanding Divine Mercy,* 43-45.

The Burning of Manuscripts

St. Margaret Mary and St. Faustina both had experiences of burning their initial manuscripts. Fr. De la Colombière ordered St. Margaret Mary to "write an account of what was taking place within me, to which I felt extreme repugnance; for I wrote only to obey." She wrote down her experiences and she thought that by doing so, she had completed her assignment and obeyed his order. Therefore, she "burnt the manuscript, thinking I had sufficiently satisfied the command given me. But I suffered much on this account, for it was made a matter of conscience to me and I was forbidden to do so again."[100]

Jesus had told St. Margaret Mary that he had granted her many graces so that "He might be glorified in the souls of those to whom I should distribute them, either by word of mouth or by writing," and that "He

---

[100] Alacoque, *Autobiography,* 85.

would add the unction of grace to my words, in order to produce the effects He wished in those who received them well."[101]

Her new *Autobiography* opened with a prayer to overcome her own resistance: "It is for the love of Thee, O my God, and through obedience, that I submit to write this account, asking Thy pardon for the resistance I have made. Thou alone knowest how great my repugnance thereto is; Thou alone therefore canst give me strength to overcome it." She continued her prayer by asking God to grant that she may write nothing but what is for "Thy greater glory and my own confusion."[102]

St. Faustina also burned her first manuscript and had to rewrite it. She had a good relationship with her spiritual director, Fr. Sopocko. Jesus had told St. Faustina not to hide anything from him, so she told him about her visions. He asked her to write them

---

[101] Alacoque, *Autobiography*, 84-85.
[102] Alacoque, *Autobiography*, 1.

down in a diary. However, she experienced temptations and attacks by demons. One demon convinced her that writing was an act of pride and went against humility, so she burned her diary. When she told this to Fr. Sopocko he asked her to rewrite it as best she could. This can make the reading of her *Diary* confusing today, because some of the records of events are not in sequential order.[103]

---

[103] Alar, *Understanding Divine Mercy,* 46-47.

The Promises of the Two Devotions

There are many promises in the accounts of Jesus's revelations to St. Margaret Mary Alacoque and St. Faustina Kowalska. There are also many benefits to the soul by practicing these devotions regularly, including establishing a regular prayer life with the Lord and reminding oneself of all He has done for us in his love and mercy.

The Sacred Heart Promises

According to Croiset, the promises of Jesus for those who practice devotion to His Sacred Heart include promises to nations, communities, families and individuals. There are promises for peace, perfection and salvation, and against the devil and sin. There are promises to draw sinners back from "the road to perdition" and to "rekindle the charity" in those who have become tepid toward the Lord. There are rewards in heaven and for people in the world, including "all the helps necessary for their state of life . . . peace in their families . . . consolation in their afflictions . . . solace in their labors . . . the blessings of Heaven . . . [and] refuge during their life and especially at the hour of their death."[104]

A number of specific promises have become associated with the devotion to the Sacred Heart, although these are not the only promises made by the Lord to St. Margaret Mary.[105] The twelve most common promises are listed below: [106]

1. "I will give them all the graces necessary in their state of life."
2. "I will establish peace in their homes."
3. "I will comfort them in their afflictions."

---

[104] Croiset, *Devotion to the Sacred Heart,* 242-249.

[105] Croiset, 242.

[106] *Holy Hour of Reparation* (Oak Lawn, IL: Marian Publishers, 2001), back cover.

4. "I will be their secure refuge during life, and above all in death."

5. "I will bestow a large blessing upon all their undertakings."

6. "Sinners shall find in My Heart the source and the infinite ocean of mercy."

7. "Tepid souls shall grow fervent."

8. "Fervent souls shall quickly mount to high perfection."

9. "I will bless every place where a picture of My Heart shall be set up and honored."

10. "I will give to priests the gift of touching the most hardened hearts."

11. "Those who shall promote this devotion shall have their names written in My Heart, never to be blotted out."

12. "I promise thee in the excessive mercy of My Heart that My all-powerful love will grant to all those who communicate on the First Friday in nine consecutive months, the grace of final

penitence; they shall not die in My disgrace nor without receiving the Sacraments; My Divine Heart shall be their safe refuge in this last moment."

The Divine Mercy Promises

There are a number of promises that have become associated with the Divine Mercy devotions. These promises are listed below, along with the relevant entries from St. Faustina's *Diary*:[107]

1. "I promise that the soul that will venerate this image (of Divine Mercy) will not perish. I also promise victory

---

[107] Wade Menezes, CPM, "Promises Attached to the Chaplet of Divine Mercy," at Fathers of Mercy (2 April 2014), at fathersofmercy.com. Excerpts taken from the *Diary* of St. Faustina Kowalska, titled *Divine Mercy in My Soul*, ©1987, Congregation of Marians of the Immaculate Conception, Stockbridge, MA 01263.

over (its) enemies already here on earth, especially at the hour of death. I Myself will defend it as My own glory." (*Diary*, 48)

2. "The souls that say this chaplet will be embraced by My mercy during their lifetime and especially at the hour of their death." (*Diary*, 754)

3. "When hardened sinners say it [the Divine Mercy Chaplet], I will fill their souls with peace, and the hour of their death will be a happy one." (*Diary*, 1541)

4. "When they say this chaplet in the presence of the dying, I will stand between My Father and the dying person, not as a just Judge but as a merciful Savior." (*Diary*, 1541)

5. "Whoever will recite it will receive great mercy at the hour of death." (*Diary*, 687)

6. "Priests will recommend it to sinners as their last hope of salvation. Even if

there were a sinner most hardened, if
he were to recite this chaplet only
once, he would receive grace from My
infinite mercy . . . desire to grant un-
imaginable graces to those souls who
trust in My mercy." (*Diary*, 687)

7. "To priests who proclaim and extol
My mercy, I will give wondrous
power; I will anoint their words and
touch the hearts of those to whom
they will speak." (*Diary*, 1521)

8. "The prayer most pleasing to Me is
prayer for the conversion for sinners.
Know, my daughter, that this prayer
is always heard and answered." (*Diary*, 1397)

9. "At three o'clock, implore My mercy,
especially for sinners; and, if only for
a brief moment, immerse yourself in
My Passion, particularly in My abandonment at the moment of agony . . .
I will refuse nothing to the soul that
makes a request of Me in virtue of My

Passion." (*Diary*, 1320; also, cf. *Diary*, 1572)

10. "Souls who spread the honor of My mercy . . . at the hour of death I will not be a Judge for them, but the Merciful Savior." (*Diary*, 1075)

11. "The two rays denote Blood and Water . . . These two rays issued from the very depths of My tender mercy when My agonized Heart was opened by a lance on the Cross. These rays shield souls from the wrath of My Father . . . I desire that the first Sunday after Easter be the Feast of Mercy . . . whoever approaches the Fount of Life on this day will be granted complete remission of sins and punishment. Mankind will not have peace until it turns with trust to My mercy." (*Diary*, 299-300)

12. "I desire that the Feast of Mercy . . . be solemnly celebrated on the first Sunday after Easter . . . The soul that will

go to Confession and receive Holy Communion (in a state of grace on this day) shall obtain complete forgiveness of sins and punishment." (*Diary*, 699)

13. "Through this chaplet you will obtain everything, if what you ask for is compatible with My will." (*Diary*, 1731)

14. "My mercy is greater than your sins and those of the entire world." (*Diary*, 1485)

The Practices of the Two Devotions

The practices that were established for both devotions form a program of activity that, like a heartbeat, can keep us focused on the Lord's generous love for us and inspire us to love Him and show mercy and love to others. The daily Chaplet of Divine Mercy reminds us that at 3:00 p.m. the Lord gave up his life on Good Friday, and it helps us to sympathize with his suffering and to recall what grateful thanks we owe him. The Holy Hour each week brings us into the presence of Jesus in adoration and encourages us to console his Sacred Heart and make reparation for those who neglect him. The practice of Communion on the first Friday of each month gives us something to look forward to each month, and provides a way to honor the Sacred Heart and prepare for the annual Feast of the Sacred Heart, which always occurs on a Friday (the one after the octave of Corpus Christi). And the Feast of Divine

Mercy, which occurs on the Sunday following Easter, invites us to embrace the Lord in his mercy and receive special forgiveness and mercy from him, regardless of what we have done, in light of his generous, forgiving and welcoming embrace of love for us. Venerating the images of the Sacred Heart and the Divine Mercy in our homes keeps our minds and hearts attuned to Jesus as our loving friend who is always with us.

All of these revelations, instructions and images which were recorded and established by two faithful nuns with their superiors and the priests who guided them, provide helpful guidance and practices by which Jesus can be more greatly known and loved. They provide the members of the Church with opportunities to understand Jesus better and worship him more intimately. The benefits for those who practice the devotions to the Sacred Heart and the Divine Mercy – praying the Divine Mercy chaplet, placing images of the Sacred Heart and Divine Mercy in their homes, visiting Jesus in the Blessed Sacrament during a holy hour each week, receiving Communion on First Fridays, and attending the feasts of the Sacred Heart and Divine Mercy – are described in many promises given by Jesus in the revelations to the saints, as listed above.

The Sacred Heart Practices

Fr. John Croiset described devotion to the Sacred Heart of Jesus as "useful, easy, reasonable and solid," and he said that it procures great graces for us."[108] The specific practices of devotion to the Sacred Heart of Jesus include those in the following list. For additional practices for every day of the year, see *The Devotion to the Sacred Heart* by Fr. John Croiset, SJ:[109]

---

[108] Croiset, *Devotion to the Sacred Heart,* 110.

[109] Croiset, *Devotion to the Sacred Heart,* 257-307.

1. Display an image of the Sacred Heart
    in your home.
2. Pray for the souls in purgatory.
3. Honor Jesus in a special way on the
    feast of the Sacred Heart.
4. Attend Mass on the first Friday of
    every month.
5. Visit Jesus in the Most Blessed Sacra-
    ment for a holy hour of reparation
    each week.
6. Consecrate yourself to the Sacred
    Heart.

Act of Consecration to the Sacred Heart
of Our Lord Jesus Christ [110]

O Lord Jesus, holy and sweet love of our
souls who hast promised that wherever
two or three are gathered together in Thy
name Thou wilt be there in their midst,

---

[110] Croiset, *Devotion to the Sacred Heart,* 311-
312.

behold, O Divine and most amiable Jesus, our hearts united in one common accord to adore, praise, love, bless and please Thy most Holy and Sacred Heart, to which we dedicate ourselves and consecrate our hearts for time and eternity. We renounce forever all love and affection which are not in the love and affection of Thy adorable Heart; we desire that all the desires, longings and aspirations of our hearts may be always according to the good pleasure of Thy Heart, which we wish to please as much as we are able. But as we can do nothing good of ourselves, we beseech Thee, O most adorable Jesus, by the infinite goodness and meekness of Thy most Sacred Heart, to sustain our hearts and confirm them in the resolution of loving and serving Thee, with which Thou dost inspire them in order that nothing may ever separate us or disunite us from Thee, but that we may be always faithful and constant in this resolution.

We sacrifice to the love of Thy Sacred Heart all that can give vain pleasure to our hearts and all that can engross them uselessly with the things of this world where we confess that everything besides loving and serving Thee alone is vanity and affliction of spirit. O Divine and most amiable Lord and Saviour Jesus Christ, may Thou be blessed, loved and glorified eternally. Amen.

The Divine Mercy Practices

The practices of devotion to the Divine Mercy may be easily remembered with the short formula, "ABC":[111]

- "A" – Ask for God's Mercy

Ask God for his mercy in prayer and in the confessional. God wants us to

---

[111] Alar, *Understanding Divine Mercy*, 26-35.

approach him, and no sin is too great. Jesus told St. Faustina that the people who sin most have a greater right to his mercy, and that if they trust in his mercy, Jesus will take on their problems and they will not perish.[112]

- "B" – Be Merciful to Others

We should be merciful to others, as God is merciful to us. In the Lord's prayer we ask God to forgive our trespasses, as we forgive those of others. We can also think of the parable of the Good Samaritan, in which Jesus described how a man helped his neighbor who had been beaten up and was lying beside the road. Two travelers passed by, but a Samaritan took him to the inn and cared for him, and then he told the innkeeper, "'Take care of him; and when I come back, I will repay

---

[112] Kowalska, *Diary,* no. 723.

you whatever more you spend.'" Jesus
then asked a lawyer, who was listening to
him tell the story, "'Which of these three,
do you think, was a neighbor to the man
who fell into the hands of the rob-
bers?' The lawyer responded, 'The one
who showed him mercy.' Jesus said to
him, 'Go and do likewise'" (Luke 10:35-
36).

Some things we can do to practice mercy
are the corporal and spiritual works of mercy.
The corporal works of mercy are actions that
tend to the practical and personal needs of
others: feed the hungry, give drink to the
thirsty, shelter the homeless, visit the sick,
visit prisoners, bury the dead and give alms to
the poor.[113]

Spiritual works of mercy address the spiritual needs of others, including teaching them

---

[113] USCCB, "The Corporal Works of Mercy,"
at www.usccb.org.

about the faith: counsel the doubtful, instruct the ignorant, admonish the sinner, comfort the sorrowful, forgive injuries, bear wrongs patiently, and pray for the living and the dead.[114]

- "C" – Completely Trust in Jesus

    Jesus told St. Faustina that he delights in people who trust in his goodness, and that the graces of his mercy are drawn to people who trust in him.[115] We can foster our trust in God's mercy by going to Confession and accepting the priest's absolution, in the person of Christ, as the endless mercy of God. We can trust in God and his love for us, and we can believe that through Jesus's atoning death on

---

[114] USCCB, "The Spiritual Works of Mercy," at www.usccb.org.

[115] Alar, *Understanding Divine Mercy*, 31-32.

the cross we are now accepted fully by God no matter what.

The specific practices of the Divine Mercy devotion include the following:[116]

1. Every day at 3:00 p.m., we can lift our hearts in a prayer of thanksgiving, remembering that it was at this hour that Jesus gave up his spirit on the cross for us.
2. Display an image of the Divine Mercy in your home to remind you of God's mercy and to increase your trust in Jesus by saying often, "Jesus I trust in You."
3. Recite the Chaplet of Divine Mercy at 3:00 p.m., as a way to remember the time Jesus died on the cross and the outpouring of God's mercy in the Redemption and in Jesus's love for us.

---

[116] Alar, *Understanding Divine Mercy,* 118.

4. Recite a novena of nine chaplets of Divine Mercy, one each day, especially from Good Friday to Holy Saturday, to place a special emphasis on certain groups of people who need God's mercy and will benefit from our prayers.

5. Participate in the Feast of Divine Mercy, which is held on the Sunday after Easter, Divine Mercy Sunday.

Conclusion

How to Blend These Devotions into Your Life

When you engage in one of these devotional practices, things may occur to you that change the course of your day. For example, I woke up from a nap in time to pray the Divine Mercy Chaplet at 3 p.m. on a Saturday. During the prayer, I was motivated – it felt like being called – to go to my Holy Hour right away, rather than waiting until the next day. This I did, and I'm here now. It's a way of hearing from Jesus that leads to more hearing from Jesus.

One thing about a holy hour of adoration is seeing the other people there, being aware of their presence. I like seeing how the "pink sisters," an order of Adoration nuns that wear pink habits, do the exchange when a new sister comes to take her place at the kneeler in front of Our Lord in the monstrance on the altar. This happens about every half hour.

The new sister emerges from a door on the right of the altar and walks silently to the nun who is kneeling. She gets up and they both bow to Jesus in the Blessed Sacrament. The new sister kneels, and the other one walks silently over to the same door and leaves. It is a quiet, gentle exchange of duties, and it disturbs no one. This is how a "peaceful transfer of power" should take place, always in service to Our Lord and the common good. The laity, too, come and go in silence. There is a reverential genuflection, usually on two knees, to honor Our Lord when someone leaves. I have been in chapels where people pray more vocally, but here it is quiet. It's a rich silence. I alternate between sitting and kneeling. When I kneel, I have a greater sense of the power of the Holy Spirit. Sometimes it's too much and I have to sit back. Other times, I spend a whole hour and do not experience this. Either way, it's okay, because I'm here with Jesus, adoring Him, offering Him reparation for my sins and those of the whole world, honoring Him and hopefully consoling Him a little, and listening for whatever He might have to say to me.

Bibliography

Alacoque, Margaret Mary. *The Autobiography of Saint Margaret Mary.* Translated by Sisters of the Visitation, Kent, England. Charlotte, NC: Tan Books, 2012.

Alar, Chris, MIC. *Understanding Divine Mercy.* Stockbridge, MA: Marian Press, 2021.

Arnoudt, Peter, SJ. *Imitation of the Sacred Heart of Jesus.* Charlotte, NC: Tan Books, 2011.

Carthusian Monks of the XIV-XVII Centuries. *Ancient Devotions to the Sacred Heart of Jesus.* Leominster, UK: Gracewing Publishing, 2018.

Croiset, John, SJ. *The Devotion to the Sacred Heart.* 2nd ed. Charlotte, NC: Tan Books, 2013.

Herbst, Clarence A., 0SJ. Introduction to *The Letters of St. Margaret Mary Alacoque.* Charlotte, NC: Tan Books, 2012.

Holy Hour of Reparation. Oak Lawn, IL: Marian Publishers, 2001.

Kowalska, St. Maria Faustina. *Diary: Divine Mercy in My Soul.* 3rd ed. Stockbridge, MA: Marian Press, 2020.

Menezes, Wade, CPM. "Promises Attached to the Chaplet of Divine Mercy." At Fathers of Mercy (2 April 2014), at fathersofmercy.com.

Michalenko, Seraphim, MIC. "Daily minutes with Fr. Seraphim Michalenko, MIC." YouTube videos, from Divine Mercy, posted on 8 September 2020. At https://www.youtube.com/c/Divine-Mercy_Official.

Michalenko, Sophia, CMGT. *The Life of Faustina Kowalska.* Cincinnati, OH: Franciscan Media, 1999.

Olsen, Kristina, PhD, DBA. *Principles of Change: Teresa of Avila's Carmelite Reform and Insights from Change Management.* St. Louis: En Route Books and Media, 2022.

Pope Pius XII. Encyclical on Devotion to the Sacred Heart *Haurietis aquas* (15 May 1956).

Ratzinger, Joseph Cardinal. *The Spirit of the Liturgy*. San Francisco: Ignatius Press, 2020.

"Saint Margaret Mary Alacoque," at Catholic Online, at https://www.catholic.org.

Stackpole, Robert A., STD. *Divine Mercy: A Guide from Genesis to Benedict XVI*. Stockbridge, MA: Marian Press, 2015.

www.ingramcontent.com/pod-product-compliance
Lightning Source LLC
Chambersburg PA
CBHW072146090426
42739CB00013B/3299